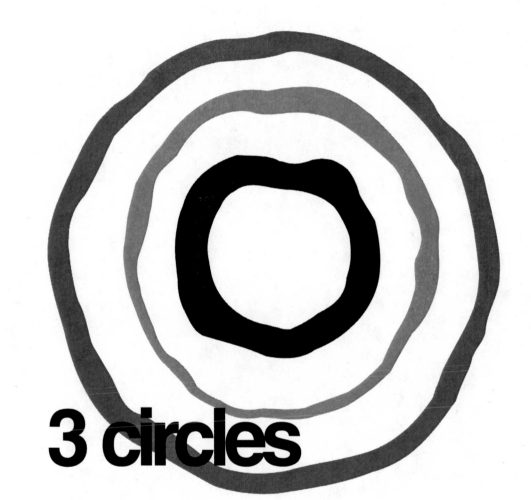

3 circles

3 circles
Mark Leuning

J. Eric Huffman: graphic design and artwork

"This is a must read! You and your church should read this work, for it will bring health and hope to all. The culture of a home or church is critical to its future and its effectiveness. Mark's book provides solid foundational truths for creating a healthy culture."

WAYNE CORDEIRO
Founder and Sr. Pastor, New Hope Christian Fellowship, Honolulu, Hawaii

"It is not often that a manuscript seems to breathe grace, yet in this short but powerful book, Pastor Mark Leuning has managed just that. His 3 Circles analogy is as clear a guide to creating a culture of grace and health as I have ever seen. Leaders, read and practice this book and your churches will never be the same."

DR. ROBERT FLORES
President, Life Pacific College

"Clear, concise and challenging, pastor Mark makes you process; culture, grace and freedom in a fresh and creative way. This short read speaks volumes. Every pastor should read this work, and then have their leaders and the church community read it. It will save them a lot of headaches and release great life."

RICHARD E. TAYLOR
Sr. Pastor, Canyon Chapel, Flagstaff, Arizona

printed in the UNITED STATES of AMERICA
ISBN - 978-0-557-85118-8

printed by www.lulu.com

author: **Mark Leuning**
graphic design and artwork: **J. Eric Huffman**

To **Jennifer**. My best friend and love. Your grace is amazing.

contents

a note to you... the reader

My primary desire in writing this book is to help both the individual and the local church. The local church community is only as strong and healthy as each individual or family unit that comprises its entirety. Though the tone and target of this writing is fundamentally intended for the local church and its leadership, which in all likelihood is my primary audience, my additional hope and prayer is that these truths will promote freedom and establish a healthy life of grace in every person who endeavors to read this book. Since the church community is only as strong as the individual who is found within, it means that as the individual goes, so also goes the family; and likewise, as families then strive to further develop and foster health and grace in their lives, so then the church community benefits and becomes an heir to that same blessing.

You will notice that throughout this book I speak honestly and straight forward about the church, in general. This comes from a very real position of having great love and passion for the church. I have enjoyed the privilege of being in and around the local church since I was three years old. To this day, I love the church and feel quite honored to have been placed in a trusted servant-role of shepherding local church bodies for over twenty five years. I believe with all my heart what Bill Hybels, the founding and senior pastor of Willow Creek Community Church, so accurately stated about the value of the church:

'The local Church is the hope of the World.'

We have the greatest opportunity at our fingertips. Right now, in our lifetime, the human cry has never been greater and the necessity for awakening never more crucial. We are called to be the hope and light to a lost and hurting

we
are meant
to be
JESUS to be
... with skin on

world, so I will fight to see the church live out loud and promote the reality of Christ, in real-time. The church is the vehicle that God has wonderfully chosen to display His grace for all to see.

We are meant to be Jesus... *with skin on.*

The layout of this book is purposefully designed to engage your heart and thoughts. Please feel free to write out your ideas, comments, thoughts and questions. Doodle and draw your own sketches. Add references to verses in scripture that help hammer home an idea or concept. We have purposefully provided abundant blank space throughout this book to accomplish this.

What you put into it, you will get out of it.

Enjoy.

introduction

It was just a small bump.

All I had felt on my neck for the previous three months had simply been a small bump, but below the surface a much larger alien had been growing. The tumor was not cancerous, but had continued to become increasingly enlarged as it grew deeper along my ear cavity, looking much like a bar bell when viewed on the MRI.

After coming through an intense four-hour surgery (and trust me, I know, any kind of surgery is intense) that was performed in order to remove the tumor on the right side of my neck, below my ear, the doctor came into my recovery room with a long, grey face. I knew immediately that he was carrying some bad news. As it happened, the surgeons had been able to remove the entire tumor, but a complication had arisen during the surgery, a complication that would affect my life deeply. I am not a doctor, but let me attempt to explain to you what had occurred in the best way I know and understand. The tumor that they found had been larger than the doctors had imagined, and it had also grown around the nerve shaft that controlled the entire right side of my face. Everybody has a web of facial nerves that spread out across each hemisphere of the face; each of us have a right side network of nerves and a left side. These microscopic cords function as pain receptors, muscle stimulators and facial expression controllers, starting as one cord below each ear on your head. The central nerve on my right side had become entangled within the tumor's growth and during surgery was beginning to show signs of stress, as the surgeons started to remove the tumor from around it. So as not to risk tearing the nerve and causing irreparable damage, they made the decision to sever the nerve cord.

it was
as if **I**
had been
punched **HARD**
in the
gut
of my **soul**

The micro-surgeon, who had been tasked with the responsibility of trying to reconnect the severed nerve after the removal of the adjacent tumor, said:

"These nerves, you know, don't come colored coded. They are the size of thin hairs... and the main nerve had three internal cords... you can't immediately distinguish a difference... it's not as if they have a blue or green or black coating."

He had done his best to sew back together all three internal cords in the correct order and then to reconnect the rest of the main nerve, believing that they would all heal somewhat over time and, perhaps, some facial feeling and expression would be restored to the right side of my face. "Mark," he said. "You will either get maybe fifty percent right-side movement back to your face... or none at all... after six months. Unfortunately, it takes the nerve about six months to regenerate. That's the best I can say for now... we will know in six months."

As I listened to the doctor's report and apology, I was completely numb (pardon the pun). The air had been knocked out of me. It was as if I had been punched hard in the gut of my soul. As I thought of not being able to smile or move my face in unison, I was in shock and just wanted to vanish from the uncomfortable encounter. I stayed a couple more days in the hospital and had yet another surgery on my eye in order to place a small sliver of gold in the eyelid, a ballast weight needed just so that it would close. With my severed nerve, the right eyelid would not be able to respond as required to close or even blink, which would cause the eye to dry out and become damaged. My eyelid would not even have been able to close for sleep.

they believed in me when I didn't believe in myself

When I finally got out of the hospital, my face looked like Rocky Balboa's face after Apollo Creed got through with him.

For some reason, however, I felt like I needed to preach that next Sunday. Call it stubborn or foolish; I wanted to get back in the saddle of my calling. In following through with that, something happened that weekend, and the several weekends that followed, that changed me forever. You have to understand, my appearance was like that of the Phantom of the Opera. One full side of my face had completely fallen slack. There was no movement, no expression; I didn't look kind or even pleasant. It was difficult for others to carry on a conversation with me; I was not a comfortable sight to behold. I had observed how people in the supermarket would take a staring second and third quick look at me... and then quickly turn away before our eyes would have a chance to fully meet. So for me to get up and teach in front of a large group of professional and well-educated people was no small task. Those first and second weeks, as I spoke the absolute-best I could out of only one side of my mouth, the words just came out slurred and labored. I constantly mispronounced the simplest of words and phrases as I struggled to make my mouth work. But despite that imperfect form of communication that I sent out, something entirely beautiful came back to me from my church community and family. Grace! They gave me their hearts and their attention; they gave me entry into their minds and souls. Though in my mind I didn't even qualify. Those precious people gave me a gift. A great and wonderful gift. The gift of grace. They believed in me when I didn't believe in myself. They embraced my fallen face and my hurting soul. That grace... that hope... that gift... was a flowing ointment that healed my heart and my soul. The emotions that had been all over the map on the inside of my life, started to find peace, comfort

GRACE does that.
it changes the hidden you, which then is revealed in the visible you.

and direction. I experienced love and grace. The real healing had begun.

There is no mistaking when you have truly tasted of grace!

Much has been spoken and written about the subject of grace. Grace is a gift. Grace is freely given to us from God; and can even be given from one person to another. It is the choice to favor, to assist or to benefit another when they don't really deserve or ask for it. For God so loved the world that he gave His only Son… God the Father graced us with the beauty and provision of His Son, Jesus Christ. He loves us so much that He offered everyone a gift of grace. This gift was the most amazing act of grace ever revealed. Grace changed our world. Grace changed countless lives and eternal futures. Real and complete grace is only found in Christ.

Just as grace is central to our relationship with God our Father, it is also necessary for each of us as we relate to one another in the community of Christ. But while grace seems easy to define, ultimately it seems much more difficult to see or experience in the Church. We know it when we receive it. We can tell when people live in it and are around it. We can invariably tell when people don't own it or know it. Many have never felt it. Far too many have never been given much grace at all. You can observe the tell-tale signs of grace-deficiency in people as they become brittle and coarse, stale and uninviting, trudging along with little joy or freedom in their lives.

I received a great dose of grace after my surgery, and that amazing gift forever changed me. Grace does that. It changes the hidden you, which then is revealed in the visible you. I truly believe that the principles and values

can you **REMEMBER** an experience of **receiving** a moment **or** season of **unexpected** or **undeserved** **favor?**

described in this book, ideas which the church first saw best modeled by our creator and have since attempted to hold dear over the years, came back to minister to me, the minister. My home church, the church I am privileged to shepherd, was living out a culture of grace, as they valued and fostered the principles found here.

So when I needed grace the most, it came and landed on me.

I invite you into a life of fresh grace.

As you read the following stories and truths, adjust your thinking, allow your heart to be stirred and believe. See your behaviors change. If you do, you will find a practical, livable understanding of grace and hope that will make it easy for you to live out real grace and love in your life, which will subsequently affect your family... and your church.

unattached
and overchurched

The statistics are in and they report that the local church in The United States of America is in crisis. These reports show that the health of the church has flat-lined in growth and conversions, and we are having little effect on our culture. The church in the U.S. is not seeing an increase of people coming to faith in Christ and, in turn, becoming His followers. I submit to you that one reason many of our churches are suffering a serious form of communal heart failure, is because at the core of our fellowships, we have become an unhealthy community. Our church culture is too often without much true passion, and yet is rife with legalism and individuals who are both aloof and out of touch with the needs of others around them. People do not find our churches to be encouraging, inclusive or even safe. They come seeking hope and honesty and all too often find instead a dry, formulized, works-oriented model infused with destructive written and unwritten rules of community.

The seeker doesn't generally have an expressed problem with Jesus; the true problem is really rooted within our man-made institutional culture and its inherent lack of life and grace.

A recent survey by The Barna Group, a California based visionary resource company dedicated to church and non-profit leadership and strategy assistance, shows that one-in-four Americans responded to a poll that they are 'born again' and believe in Christ-- but are 'unattached' when it comes to pairing this faith with physical church attendance and involvement. They belong to no church community, nor do they make church-life a regular function of their personal lifestyle. These "unattached" individuals, as Barna describes, are turned-off by the culture we have created and the values we press into the framework our churches. My experiences working within the

church culture, as I have been pastoring over the last twenty-five years, is that many of these 'unattached' have become disenchanted of any involvement because they have actually been, what I would term, 'overchurched.' The overchurched are those who once came to a saving knowledge of Jesus Christ and began to find a place within their local church, but after a time, they witnessed enough unhealthy relationships, pride and ego in leadership, and overt legalism in church practices, that they no longer felt a desire to participate or continue within the community. They witnessed an alarming situation where the 'ministry' is more important than people.

This is not Jesus. This is not the healthy community which God the Father intended.

The very ground, or soil, of the church fellowship has become toxic, unhealthy, and unable to sustain life and must be plowed and altered if it is to survive.

life attracts life

When a healthy church culture is established, it nurtures hope and security, and when this 'green' environment is maintained, the church community will experience growth. This growth will be positive, dynamic and secure. Individuals will leave behind their brokenness and pain as they come to faith in Christ. Life attracts life. While inevitably the overall attendance numbers will increase, more importantly, this physical growth is accompanied by very personal, spiritual, maturing growth.

How can this happen?

How can just changing the culture or soil of the church make such a radical difference?

Historically, much of church-growth teaching and information has focused on technique, style, or a certain program of implementation that churches are advised to follow in order to see growth. While well-intentioned and often helpful, these concepts and ideas have not generally addressed the real issue. Too often, they may have simply added water to a diseased soil. The real issue is the innate DNA or core culture of the church. This core culture contains the non-visible atmosphere and climate of the fellowship, its internal relational and emotional health; it is the fundamental life source of the churches' ecosystem. A church culture permeates all that you do and offer as a community. The church culture and its atmosphere will effectively transcend what is being preached and taught. The culture sticks with people far longer than what is heard. What people pick up in heart and spirit is more acute and discernible to them, and thus more powerful in affecting their values and choices.

could it be that culture, and atmosphere TRANSCEND word and deed?

After each service I always create an opportunity to make myself available to meet the guests or families that are "checking us out" or visiting our church campus. In these encounters, I have often received unsolicited statements that shouldn't surprise me, but they do every single time. As we greet and exchange names, these new guests will volunteer statements, not typically about the building... or the message (which was very good, by the way)... or the inspiring music... but, really, about the culture of our church. All too often, a guest will express, in one form or another, statements such as: "There is real hope in this place;" or "I felt like I was home;" or "you seem to be a church that loves each other and are really devoted to God;" or "this place has a lot of life and joy;" or "I really enjoyed the freedom to just be me."

Why is that?

Why are they not inherently impressed with the worship songs we worked so hard to express with excellence? Or why are they not sufficiently challenged or encouraged by the empowering message that was one of a kind? What they are describing is atmosphere-- the environment or the culture-- not the obvious elemental components of the service. How can they know this in one visit? How do they pick this up in one hour?

Could it be that culture and atmosphere transcend word and deed?

While these things have often been true of our church, it never ceases to amaze me what people really pick up and grab hold of. It has been said, "More is caught than taught." People really seem to easily pick up on our dearly held unseen values and motives far more than the music we choose or

how could you IMPROVE the kind of culture or atmosphere that you project or foster?

the words we use. This "more is caught than taught" axiom is a potent reality; so, to be sure, the first place we must consider and maintain in our church is its culture – its climate – its atmosphere.

Where does the culture of a church originate?

What is the beginning point or starting strata of this atmosphere?

the word says

In the Gospels of both Matthew and Mark, we find two passages that give great insight into the reality and power of a healthy culture:

"Now here is the explanation of the story I told about the farmer sowing grain: The seed that fell on the hard path represents those who hear the Good News about the Kingdom and don't understand it. Then the evil one comes and snatches the seed away from their hearts. The rocky soil represents those who hear the message and receive it with joy. But like young plants in such soil, their roots don't go very deep. At first they get along fine, but they wilt as soon as they have problems or are persecuted because they believe the word. The thorny ground represents those who hear and accept the Good News, but all too quickly the message is crowded out by the cares of this life and the lure of wealth, so no crop is produced. The good soil represents the hearts of those who truly accept God's message and produce a huge harvest — thirty, sixty, or even a hundred times as much as had been planted."
[Matthew 13:18-23]

The words of Jesus in this passage describe the seed of the Gospel as it is sown into three types of soil. Take notice that this parable gives us insight not about the seed, but the soils. The makeup of the soil is vital to the long term health of the seed and the impending developing plant. Good soil will produce fruit in great numbers.

In the Gospel of Mark we find another fascinating teaching. Jesus also said, this parable gives us INSIGHT not about the seed, but the SOILS.

"Here is another illustration of what the Kingdom of God is like: A farmer planted seeds in a field, and then he went on with his other activities. As the days went by, the seeds sprouted and grew without the farmer's help, because the earth produces crops on its own...."
[Mark 4:26-28]

In these passages Jesus is explaining that when the soil is healthy, growth will happen. Jesus related in the parable found in Mark that the seed will spring up all by itself. Natural, or may I say super-natural, life and growth will take place with fruit-to-follow, when the seed is planted in a good healthy soil.

God is telling us in these scriptures about natural biotic principles – if the ground is healthy and rich with balanced nutrients, the plant will grow strong and bring forth fruit, as it is designed to do. The emphasis and priority being taught is not about where the soil is placed or how it looks or the style the soil projects, but is about the very fabric or goodness (health) of the soil.

What does the seed find when it falls into, or is placed, in the ground?

Is the soil and culture one of grace, life and benefit; or is it one that is rocky, unprotected, and crammed with convoluted values? The local church is, by the Father's great design, intended to be a rich and vibrant soil, where many seeds can find a place of health, hope and growth, where they will germinate into plants that bear much fruit.

habitat
for health

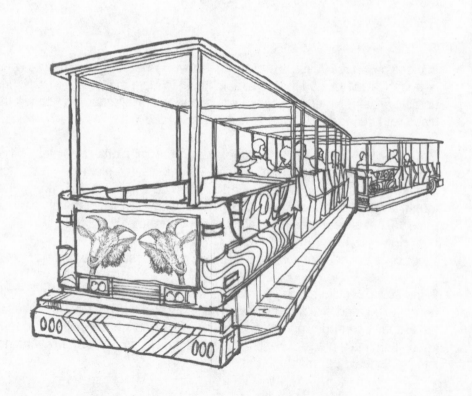

One of my friends attended a wild animal park and related to me this story that gives great insight into this principle of healthy culture and environment.

He got on board a tram that traveled through the breadth of a local wild animal park. This tram would visit each of the large and extensive habitats built for the different species. As they traversed the park, the guide explained extensive details about each wild animal encountered. A number of these habitats were projects conducted in conjunction with other countries and zoos to save animals from all over the world from possible extinction. The tour eventually happened upon a habitat of New Guinea Goats that were there on loan from another zoo. The guide mentioned that these Goats were not happy at all and were, actually, somewhat depressed. My friend wondered how one could tell when a goat is unhappy or depressed? Do they not smile? Are they grumpy to others somehow? So he raised his hand and asked the guide,

"How do you know if they are unhappy goats?"

The park guide responded, "Great question. Well, this is how we know – they have been here for over a year, and not one of them has become pregnant. In our research we have found that happy, healthy animals naturally reproduce. Something is clearly wrong in the goats' environment. We potentially have the wrong surroundings or food or shelter. We need to make a change and quickly, because we could easily lose them all."

Happy, healthy followers of CHRIST WILL reproduce, making more followers

There it is.
We are just like New Guinea Goats in a zoo.

Happy, healthy followers of Christ will reproduce, making more followers. Healthy churches will grow! A happy, healthy church will attract others to come alongside and foster "new babies" in faith. This process is just natural. If we can bring health and happiness to goats, we can surely, with the grace of God and the power of His Spirit, find the factors in our church environment that need to be altered to produce life and health. Clearly something is unhealthy in many of our churches. But by adjusting the habitat, the very atmosphere and culture of our church community, we can see noticeable signs of life, new babies, new believers in Christ, and natural reproduction by relational evangelistic growth. Our environment, our culture needs to be changed. All of our habitats need to have an inspection; if any signs of disease or neglect are found, then our habitats need an overhaul.

a better way

A certain church fellowship is about to blow up and tear apart.

Hair, teeth and eyeballs will be all that is left of this once-great church, with a previously amazing history of mission's outreach and worship expression. Effective ministry has been replaced with seismic currents of anger, resentment and passionate conviction flowing through polarizing statements being made by its fractionating members. The church business meeting continues this implosion, and this church is seemingly now only headed for a major meltdown. These good, Godly people are fighting... over petty and insignificant concerns. The unavoidable outcome of all this explosive emotion is that many people will be hurt and many others will leave and never come back. Worse still, others, most painfully, will walk away and ultimately question their entire basis of faith.

How did it get this way?

Unfortunately, this is a true story, and is too often repeated in cities and towns just like yours and mine. This might even be your church.

I heard recently of a church that had been in the midst of a remodeling project of the main chapel, or sanctuary, and they became embroiled in fighting and clawing over whether to purchase pews or chairs, or try to keep the old ones that had worn out. The founding pastor had originally had the conviction that instead of chairs, the church should keep the old pews and send the money that would have been spent on new chairs to missions. Today, years later, the founding pastor has gone home to heaven, and the church has been trying to move forward. But because the pastor had previously made his personal

the culture
must be changed
if
the church
community is to SURVIVE
and once again thrive

preference part of the churches' culture, by pressing his conviction into what amounted to a Biblical absolute in the minds of the people in his church, crisis and pain ultimately resulted. While this should never be the case, it too often is. The culture of this church has become tainted and brittle and thus has lost sight of its main purpose-- to be people who show the love of Christ to the world by how they love each other and then bring the Good News of Jesus to others. The culture must be changed if the church community is to survive and once again thrive. It has to be healed and renewed to match the heart of our Savior. Too many have experienced this repeating history of heartache in the local churches they have attended, adding brick by brick to the wall built entirely of a person's disillusionment and discouragement.

We can avoid much of the hardship and pain in the lives of the church family and its leaders if we can learn to understand and follow a system of categorizing how we classify and ultimately respond to issues that permeate the fabric of our lives.

This is what I call "The Three Circles."

3 circles:
the center circle
the biblical core

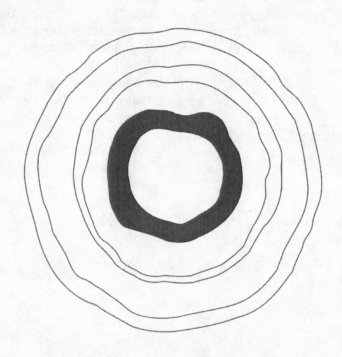

The center circle is where we find the core of Biblical absolutes in our Christian life. These are items that we would classify as non-negotiable. They are the very foundational elements of our faith in God. These are the life-transforming principles of God's love, life and His Word. They are not suggestions or opinions; they are God's truth and reality. A few examples follow:

- *The Bible is God's word, inspired by the Spirit; His truth and heart expressed to us.*

- *The Trinity of the Godhead, the Father, Son and Holy Spirit, are each eternal, holy and divine.*

- *There is one God alone, only one God without beginning or end.*

- *Jesus Christ is the only begotten Son of the Father and is truly God. He is the way of salvation and eternal life.*

- *We are saved by grace through faith, not of works, through the atoning work of the cross.*

- *Only by the blood of Jesus Christ can one be forgiven and redeemed.*

- *We are to fulfill the heart of God by loving Him with all our body, soul, mind and spirit and to love our neighbor as ourselves.*

These are just some examples of the core of our Christianity, the Biblical truths we follow and the teachings of Christ we desire to live out. I will refer to more specific beliefs later in the book.

3 circles:
the second circle
personal convictions + traditions

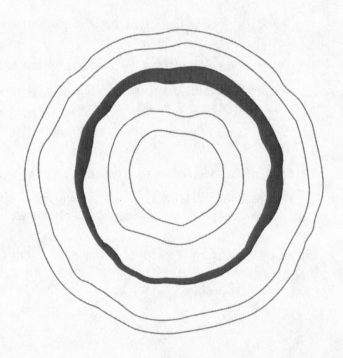

The second circle is the realm where we hold our personal convictions and traditions. We all should have personal convictions and traditions. These are the values and issues we hold with passion and strength of heart. Each church, family, and individual has them and should be encouraged to develop personal convictions and traditions. Some examples of personal convictions and traditions could be:

- *An individual may have convictions about what he or she will or will not eat.*

- *A conviction might dictate what one will watch on TV or what rating of movie they will enjoy.*

- *A family might have convictions about what means of education is right for their family, such as home-schooling, public school or private school.*

- *There are those who have convictions about their choice of attire, whether they will or will not wear certain clothing.*

- *Personal convictions and traditions can include which specific Bible translation an individual or church will choose.*

- *People have strong personal convictions and traditions about politics - who they will vote for, who they will not vote for, what issues are of importance, what party holds their values.*

Families develop and have traditions that are meaningful to them and hold a certain value and memory; and churches have the same ability to hold onto traditions. Personal convictions are just that - personal and thus passionate.

As well they should be.

These values and passionate choices are to be encouraged and given room, not discouraged or disqualified. Personal convictions should be encouraged and enjoyed by each church, family and person.

In the local church fellowship we should applaud and champion people in striving for and maintaining their personal convictions. This is what makes for variety and life. People who live out their convictions are too often few and far between, and the church needs more, not fewer, people of conviction.

"In the same way, some think one day is more holy than another day, while others think every day is alike. Each person should have a personal conviction about this matter."
[Romans 14:5]

3 circles:
the third circle
personal preference

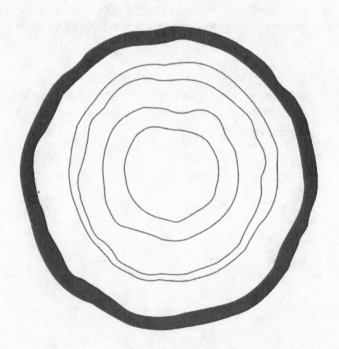

This outer circle, the third circle, is where we tend to hold our preferences and leanings. This is what you prefer to do or enjoy in your activities and lifestyle. For instance:

- *If you go to the movies you may have the personal conviction to see only PG rated shows (second circle), your personal preference would be what type of PG rated shows you like to enjoy, such as a romantic comedy or action or drama. The style or genre of the film is your personal preference.*

- *A family has a conviction (second circle) to home school their children, but the choice of materials used in the education process is their personal preference.*

These personal preferences are amoral and subjective, differing one person to another, from one church to another. Some individuals prefer country music; some prefer classical; others would rather enjoy soft rock. Some churches prefer drums as part of their worship music, and some do not care for them at all. Others like drums as well as chimes and other percussion instruments. All types differing styles and aesthetics come under this circle. Be it an individual, family or a church, each has unique personal preferences which are to be embraced, enjoyed and celebrated.

In the chapters ahead, I will give insight into how we live out a clear understanding of these Three Circles and, in doing so, create and foster a grace-oriented life as an individual, family and church.

'65 VW

I was winding through the hills and valleys of Marin County, 40 miles north of San Francisco, California, in my '65 VW Bug, acting like it was a Porsche Carrera GT, down-shifting and leaning into every curve. The windows were down and the wind, combined with the warm sunshine coming through the glass washed over me, bringing a touch of life and joy to my soul. The car radio was turned up and pumping out the sounds of years past, the dial was set on the station which played the Golden Oldies. It was spring and we were beginning to see the fruit of our having planted a church in this area two years earlier.

Life was good.

I was on my way to take a new Christian believer to lunch. Steve had just begun to follow Jesus Christ, and I had the privilege of being the one who got to be there to gather the harvest, where others had previously planted and watered this seed of faith. One afternoon, just a few weeks before, Steve and I had prayed together and he received Jesus Christ as his Savior and Lord in faith. Steve's personal history was one full of the excess of parties, women and drugs, since his teens. He had been known as a "key player" for his lifestyle of extremes and for owning and running the best burger hangout in town. Steve, now in his late thirties, was starting a whole new way of life.

I pulled up at the curb right outside his restaurant, and Big Steve (that's what everybody called him) with all 6 feet 4 inches of his football lineman barrel-chested frame, squeezed himself into the passenger side of the pastor's "nice" car. I fired up the Bug, the radio came to life and I pulled away. Once underway, with the tunes turned somewhat down, I figured we could talk.

I started with small talk. Steve would respond, but only with short curt statements. We only had about a twenty minute drive before arriving at our destination for lunch, but I could tell something was definitely wrong. The farther we drove, the more Steve shrunk into his seat and looked away out the window, becoming detached. The color started to go from his face, and it was obvious that he was more and more uncomfortable.

I asked straight out, "Steve, what's wrong? Are you doing ok?"

He didn't really respond at first. He looked at me and then out the window. He actually looked as if he might throw up. I slowed the car down and encouraged him again. "Seriously, you can tell me, what's goin' on?"

Finally, after some more awkward silence, he sighed and then said, "Pastor, this is really just very uncomfortable for me."

"What is? Going to lunch?" I asked, very much puzzled.

"No! Not that at all. I never really even thought this would be a problem for me before, but this... this is not good for me..."

Steve shut down again and he actually seemed even more irritated.

My mind raced to find a clue. I couldn't put my finger on it. What was so troubling to him? What was he concerned about? I could see he was searching for the right words and thoughts so as not to offend or jeopardize this new friendship. Finally, after a few minutes of awkward silence, the dam over the next few days, the HOLY SPIRIT began to teach me from this valuable encounter completely broke.

"Pastor Mark," he said, with deep respect and emotion, "I just can't listen to this music! It brings up all kinds of bad images, thoughts and stuff. Like this song playing right now reminds me of a time I was out getting loaded with a bunch of friends. We would listen to that song as we partied. The song that was just playing before this one actually brought back memories of having sex and smoking pot. I am sorry, I really can't do this right now."

I was cut to the core.

I immediately turned off the radio with as quick a twist of my hand as I could deliver. I then spoke clearly and honestly to Steve.

"Steve, that will never happen again. I am so sorry I have caused you to be offended and that my listening to that music brought up all that trash from your past to your mind. Please, forgive me. I want you to know that it was never my intention to bring these experiences up for you again. I really appreciate you making me aware of your feelings and thoughts."

Over the next few days, the Holy Spirit began to teach me from this valuable encounter. In prayer and in the quietness of my soul, I began to learn, as a young church-planting pastor, more about the application of the concept of three circles to my life and those around me. My personal preference of music (third circle) had been tripping up this young believer and bringing about a stumbling block, an offense, which cast a remorseful and guilty point in his mind to his past. Though I did not know it at the start, my choice at that

the **second**
AND **third** circles
always **yield**
to the **BIBLICAL**
core

time was not appropriate, loving or healthy.

The Bible is quite clear on this.

"If what I eat is going to make another Christian sin, I will never eat meat again as long as I live — for I don't want to make another Christian stumble."
[1 Corinthians 8:13]

Be it meat or music, the Biblical core of love and preferring one another always must trump one's personal conviction or personal preference. I didn't have a personal conviction about the oldies music station. But even if I had, that was not the issue. It was my personal preference of music, and for me, listening to this type of music was not a sin. It didn't bring up past life issues or cause me to stumble. The style of music is amoral. It was not sin then, or now. It was not the devil's music. Some of those songs are even sweet poems of love and devotion arranged to a melodic voice. But, it would be a sin to push my preference upon Steve when it caused him so much pain. I would be violating the core circle.

As soon as my personal preference (or personal conviction) could cause another to doubt, question or stumble in their faith, it must stop. The second and third circles must always yield to the Biblical core, not the other way around. We must choose to live from the core principles out. Thus love and grace, safety and courage remain densely tilled into the soil of the culture. Any individual or church culture will thrive when it maintains these proper boundaries and consistently acts upon them. They must act to keep them present and understood and act to defend them, keeping the circles from

what
conduct
do you
have
that could cause
another
CHRISTIAN
to stumble
or
create doubt?

becoming weakened or misapplied.

My sensitivity to others' backgrounds and to their personal experiences was increased immensely the day of that car ride. I have a greater awareness of my surroundings and my personal antennas are better tuned to pick up on possible points of offense. I want to be known as one who heals, encourages, strengthens, and builds up; not one who would knowingly cause confusion, conflict or pain for another follower of Christ.

circles and grace

Later, I was able to communicate to Steve the important lesson we both were learning that spring day in the '65 VW Beetle. I shared with him about my choice that day to love and protect his young relationship with Christ. I explained that I am the one who should defer to him, for I know better, have had more learned experience in the arena of becoming free and am to be the one to set an example. It is for me to adjust and change my behavior, not him. We discussed that the way of love and choosing the core principles over personal preference is always honoring to God. I encouraged him to be aware of possible concerns in fellow believers and to learn to take the higher way of love in his interactions with others. He also needed to keep a clear understanding that he is absolutely free to have and hold personal convictions and preferences, but to keep those in submission to the Biblical core of God's truth. What a liberating time we had as we talked together and I was able to relate to Steve some of these concepts which would help him walk out his salvation with hope, confidence and a healthy freedom. He needed to hear that my personal preference of music was not a sin or something evil. That this style of music was fine for me on a personal level, even though it was not for him, and that this kind of circumstance will eventually happen to him as he interacts with others of faith.

Steve found great hope and security as we discussed and listened to each other, and so did I.

Any follower of Christ needs to know that because of individuals' experiences, backgrounds and levels of maturity, there will always be a variety of styles, convictions and preferences, within the body of Christ. It is good for us to realize and accept that God's design for His family was not for everyone to be

this **key**
principle
brings **a**
livable understanding
to **Christians**
for **REAL** everyday
sustainable
HEALTH

just a bunch of cookie-cutter Christians with the same mantra and look. We have an assortment of overcoming testimonies, each one carrying an innate ability to influence a certain circle of lives with the message and grace of our Savior, Jesus.

Having a clear understanding of when to release grace, letting things go, and when to prayerfully cover or approach another, would be paramount for Steve as he walked out his Christianity in the human arena. We are always to give grace to another's actions of immaturity. Immaturity is not sin. We are to give grace, which is to give space and room, to believe the best and support the person. For "love covers a multitude of sins," especially when dealing with issues of immaturity. People have differing preferences and convictions, and as long as these various values do not violate the Biblical core truths, they are to be given grace and covered by our love, one for another. Grace and love are to be given to others in any actions that come from the outer two circles.

This key principle brings a livable understanding to Christians for real everyday sustainable health. It works! A person affronts God's heart when a personal conviction/tradition or personal preference violates the core Biblical circle.

When an individual purposely chooses to disobey one of God's love commands or Biblical absolutes, he or she misses the core target and thereby sins. (The historic meaning of sin was when an archer would miss the bulls-eye and the on-looking crowd would yell, "Sin!") When this happens, the person's relationship with Christ will lose heart and passion and begin to falter. Sin brings about brokenness, loss and death. We should respect and love each other enough to speak the truth (the Biblical core circle) in love when we see

this happening.

The Bible clearly states these practices in the following scriptures:

"Instead, speaking the truth in love, we will in all things grow up into him who is the Head, that is, Christ."
[Ephesians 4:15]

"My dear brothers and sisters, if anyone among you wanders away from the truth and is brought back again, you can be sure that the one who brings that person back will save that sinner from death and bring about the forgiveness of many sins."
[James 5:19-20]

hats or hearts

After service one Sunday morning, I was told by one of our staff pastors that we seemed to have a problem with one of the church council members. I immediately met with the council member, Robert, in my office, and at first glance he was noticeably upset and irritated. His face angrily flushed and the veins bulged from his neck as he very emotionally launched into a description of an encounter he had just experienced that now left him with the unshakable certainty that we had young people in the church service that day that absolutely needed to change their ways!

"Pastor, they were wearing their baseball caps inside the sanctuary during our time of worship and prayer... you know what I'm talking about... those black ball caps turned around backwards. It was just not right! They need to learn to have the proper respect for the house of God... and that means learning to take those hats off when they come inside. They weren't going to do it on their own, so I did it for them."

"You did what?" I asked.

"I took their caps right off their heads and slapped them into their chests... I said to them, 'Not in here. Have respect.'"

I calmed myself from reacting and spoke to Robert in a clear steady tone.

"Robert, do you remember the whole discussion regarding the concept of the three circles that was taught in the newcomer's orientation class?"

"Well, sure I do." Robert replied.

the **LORD** doesn't see **things** the way **you** SEE them.

people **JUDGE** by outward appearance, but the **LORD** looks at the **heart**

1 SAMUEL 16:7

"Okay, just so that we're on the same page here, let me review that whole idea for just a moment. Remember that the center circle is the area associated with Biblical core absolutes, the second circle is where your personal convictions are located and then the outer third circle is the zone of all things that are your personal preferences. Robert, I can tell that this issue of wearing baseball caps, or hats of any kind, in church is of importance to you. It really seems to be a personal conviction to you, correct?"

"Yes, I would say that is true."

With compassion but firmness in my voice, I further challenged him. "You know, I really am glad you have that conviction, and I certainly respect your heart in this matter... I really do. But you can't let your personal conviction ever become a Biblical core absolute. The Bible is very clear that God does not find it important to look at the heads of people to see what they are or are not wearing, but what he does find important is that he looks at what is in their heart. He is far more interested in that. You have taken this personal conviction of yours and elevated it to a position of it being a Biblical core absolute. And now... as a result of your decision, it has been received by others as being a Biblical core absolute in this church. You have to know that this kind of intrusion into the center circle will always kill God's love and grace to you... and others. Do you remember at the newcomer's orientation when I said that we as a church together would hold to these truths and walk them out in real life... so that to the best of our ability we will never let any personal conviction or personal preference ever become a Biblical core absolute?"

neither **you** nor **I** are to **stand** in the **way** of the **most** important **decision** of their **LIVES**

"Well, yes, I guess I do remember you saying that. And Yes, I agree with you and want that!" Robert stated with some feeling.

"Do you see what took place in this encounter you had with those boys today?"

"Actually, yes, I do see what you're saying. I really just let my personal conviction overrun and hurt others. I guess I let my emotions get the best of me."

With a softer tone and a spirit of true personal concern, I responded to him.

"Robert, I see that you are humbled and open to seeing this important lesson. I also have to let you know this: I would absolutely love to see our church filled to capacity with baseball-cap wearing students in every service, if that's what God wants to do. That is one of the most important reasons we even exist as a church, we are here to reach people. You need to know that this is a premier ministry focus and passion around here. Remember, the Biblical core in this situation is that God looks at the heart... and not the outside. The Holy Spirit is moving these students to hear and receive the Good News of Jesus Christ. Neither You nor I are to stand in the way of the most important decision of their lives. Robert, I don't want to hear about this happening again. You are a church leader and have the privileged responsibility of setting the tone for the attitude and values we hold dearly here at The Springs. Do you agree with this?

Robert spoke with a touch of grace and heartfelt change.
"Yes, Pastor. I am sorry for the way that I reacted... and I will walk this out. I

in your experience, what are a couple of other 'hat' moments that have HURT the purpose of the church?

love the heart we have here at this church for people."

"Let's pray."

We did.
As I stood up, he came around the table and hugged me.

the
prime directive

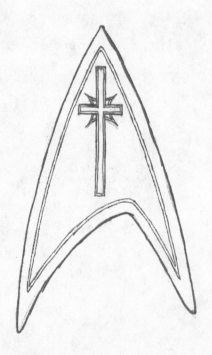

Besides its many intriguing characters and fascinating story lines, the TV show Star Trek was a ground breaking series that changed the face of television and created a cult following. One of the intriguing aspects of the TV series was that as a part of the show's premise, the characters had certain principles and values that were required to be adhered to within the context of their continuing encounters with other beings as they toured the universe in the episodes from week to week.

One such core belief was their obedience to following "The Prime Directive."

Simply stated, the Prime Directive was a code of conduct in which all U.S.S. Enterprise officers and crewmen would not interfere with any aspect of another culture that they met. Over the course of their five-year voyage, they would encounter numerous species and planetary scenarios, and regardless of the parameters of that experience, they were not allowed to engage that race, culture or planet in such a way that would alter or change its future.

Likewise, we also have a Prime Directive on our lifelong voyage with the Creator. We are to hold true to the Biblical core absolute – center circle - of our Christianity. This means that we are to live in such a way as to give grace to all of the various personal convictions and traditions we find around us, all the while not fostering or allowing the Biblical absolutes to be derailed by letting personal convictions or traditions steal the joy of living in the Spirit.

A healthy culture and environment is established when the three circles are maintained and lived-out with clarity and purpose. Where we find leaders who wholly defend the core from being polluted by the invasion of personal a healthy environment &culture is established when the three circles are maintained and lived-out with clarity + purpose convictions, there we will find safety and hope. In this type of garden, the 'overchurched' will come to a place of freedom and life. This works at both an individual level, as well as, the corporate church level. The church community that acknowledges and fosters the separation and practice of classifying preferences, convictions and absolutes into the categorization of the three circles cannot help but release an atmosphere of grace and empowerment. The people will have for themselves something they can rely upon, a healthy culture, a good 'rock free' soil, where they can freely embrace life in the Spirit as they walk in grace and hold fast to the core Biblical truths.

When this type of community is found – look out, World!

fiddler
on the roof

Have you ever wondered how the style of music, the use of instruments (or even the lack of use), the order of a service or even the employment of a certain Bible translation can become such an embedded tradition and such a strong passionate point of identity within a church's reality? These types of traditions can cause even otherwise Godly people to vociferously fight one another over perceived differences in the view of these ideals, ultimately causing major division and conflict within the local fellowship.

Traditions can become so strong and personalized that they move out of the realm of being helpful concepts to becoming instead (fraudulent) Biblical core absolutes in the hearts and minds of the people.

Here is how this type of scenario unfolds and can become a reality in many churches. The church starts out with a right-hearted intention, goal or desire of taking some positive steps towards a new direction or area of growth. The leadership and the people choose to take calculated steps of action and faith for the ultimate purpose of attempting to increase the church's overall health and life. Then, the pastor and the church leadership, while flushing out the new direction, simply inject a personal preference into the life of the church community. It may be as innocuous as the decision to use a certain kind of music or the desire to have all the people read from the New International Version Bible translation. It could be that the pastor thinks it best to pray at a specific point during each worship service. As this preference brings benefit and fruit, it moves into the next circle of becoming a conviction for that church or leadership. Once it enters this realm, the longer it continues without being changed or altered, it gently becomes a tradition.

What wonderful traditions have you ENJOYED in your church or worship experience?

When a pastor models a personal conviction with regard to liturgy, style of music or a prayer formula, and if it remains in place, over time it easily can take on a life and history of its own. We have all heard the lines within a community or organization: "that's how we do it around here;" or "Let's just keep it that way;" or "Don't try to change it, it works." Eventually, this tradition, when solidly cemented in the minds and hearts of the church fellowship, primarily due to their love, esteem and rightful submission to the pastor's authority will be interpreted by everyone involved as a non-negotiable Biblical core value. It is unfortunately seen, and implied, as something that God would want the fellowship to always do or hold dear.

That is the possible path of travel that an outer third circle personal preference can take as it penetrates into the center Biblical core. Whenever we move a personal preference or a personal conviction/tradition into the core, we will unavoidably encounter legalism. We will also experience the wilting of grace and life.

We have all seen this to be true. We have all heard stories or have been part of this scene. Just look at a church going through a pastoral change after having had a successful pastor lead them for a number of years. It can be very ugly. But it doesn't have to be.

Let us agree that traditions and order are wonderful and valuable assets. But the fellowship of believers must be taught and reminded that these assets are for the benefit of the moment and meant to serve us. We are not to serve them. They are not absolutes. We won't die for these personal preferences or convictions. These are tools and styles that help us bring the message of the message never changes, but the methods can and will

Jesus and His grace to people.

We need to create a culture where these traditions can be fostered and used, but also easily set aside, altered or adjusted to make way for new and fresh approaches to ministering the Gospel. We must never allow a tradition, rooted in personal preference or personal conviction, to become the Biblical core in the minds or practice of our churches.

The message never changes, but the methods can and will. Balanced and healthy leadership understands this. In fact, true leadership actually allows for, and leads in such a way, that the methods are tweaked occasionally; genuine space is created to allow for the option of utilizing new forms of relating the Good News, whether in the style of worship, the order of service or the manner in which we preach the Word.

keep
quiet and listen

The morning church service was over and conversation, mixed with laughter, filled the air as families and individuals interacted in the church lobby. A man in his mid-twenties named Thomas approached me with a bounce in his step and a countenance of pure joy. Thomas was new to our church family; also a brand-new follower of Christ. It had been only two weeks since he had asked for his sins to be forgiven and had accepted the love and power of Jesus into his heart and life. He was learning so much and had so much to learn. The smile on his face and the experience of fresh life in his eyes could not be contained any longer and from his lips, burst: "Pastor Mark, I was baptized last night in my apartment!"

"Wow, that's great." I was just a little surprised and shocked. "Uh, tell me about it."

His words came shooting out in rapid choppy statements. "Well, I was reading in the New Testament - like you told me to do - and I came across the time that they were - I think it was in John - baptizing people who wanted their sins forgiven - because they wanted to know God. And I thought to myself – well, I want all my sins forgiven - I want to do this - this is for me. I want to be freed from all my sins – I want to have them washed away. They would enter the river, Pastor Mark - and were being baptized – so I thought, how can I do this right now?"

As Thomas was sharing this exciting event in his life, I was listening to him and my mind was also thinking *I really like this guy's childlike heart and desire to obey God.*

don't say a **thing.**

don't you

dare

try to
fix **this**

or

straighten him
out...

keep

QUIET!

His understanding might be a little off, so I will just try to correct...
The Holy Spirit interrupted my thoughts and poked me in my heart and said to me, "Don't say a thing. Don't you dare try to fix this or straighten him out on the proper way to be baptized. Keep Quiet!"

Thomas continued. "So I got up from my chair and with all my clothes on I turned on the shower and just jumped in! I prayed, 'Jesus, please wash me from the top of my head to the bottom of my feet. Wash all of the past and sin away.' Something happened in that shower. I could tell. That was so awesome! What do you think of that?"

Another soft nudge by the Spirit: "See the heart and faith he has extended to me – I am pleased!"

I pushed back my theological arguments regarding proper baptism methodology and how it should be done with full immersion and witnesses. I decided, instead, to listen to the still small voice, to hear the sweet melody of faith and heart.

"Thomas, that is just wonderful. I love your act of obedience and openness of heart to God. That's fantastic. Clothes-n-all, that must have been a real joy..."

Thomas interrupted. "But Pastor, afterwards, I also noticed in the Gospel that it described that those entering the water to be baptized told about their sins publicly and confessed before others. How does that work? Pastor, should I do that too?"

where do **you** need to remain **quiet** and **trust** the **HOLY SPIRIT** to **work?**

Oh Lord, I am so glad I listened!

"Thomas, you are right. Numerous times in scripture we have the example of baptism as a public confession of a believer's faith in Christ and a turning from their past life of sin. Is that something you would like to do, to invite your family, friends and have them see you commit publicly to your new life in Christ?"

"Yes I would!"

"Great! Then we can set a time in the next couple weeks and do just that. Why don't you and I have lunch this week and we can do some more Bible study on baptism and its importance to us, as believers. Does that sound good?"

"Yes, that would be amazing. I really know God is working and changing me... and this baptism thing is cool."

I couldn't agree more, I thought to myself.

I learned a powerful lesson that morning. If I had jumped in, stepped on his story and showed him the 'proper and official' way to really be baptized, I could have smashed his faith and quenched the heart and spirit of God's working in Thomas. I might have accomplished doing the 'correct' thing by doing that, but I would not have been 'right;' I would have been completely wrong.
At times, we can be entirely correct and still be wrong.

...the faith and heart of a person in obedience to hearing the voice of GOD trumps our method of sacrament

The Biblical core absolute of entering the Kingdom of God with childlike faith was clearly in operation within Thomas. I could have crushed that childlike faith. I might have said something like, "Thomas that's a good start, not entirely the right thing... but let me tell you what the Bible really says and how you really need to be baptized." He might have completely lost the joy and perspective of instant obedience and the personal testimony of the Holy Spirit ministering directly to him. Doubt and a second-guessing of his ability to hear and respond to God may have settled in on him.

How often have I mistakenly done this? How often do we do this in our churches by crushing or stifling faith and grace by blindly pronouncing our convictions and values, which in turn, run right over the heart of Biblical core truth?

Anytime we place a personal conviction/tradition or personal preference at the core, as a Biblical truth, we surely kill grace and life and quench the Spirit.

Now, please do not misunderstand me. I believe very strongly about the method of baptism we use in our church fellowship. It is founded upon scripture and we teach it to our people. But, I also believe that the faith and heart of a person in obedience to hearing the voice of God trumps our method of sacrament. Thomas truly believed he was being baptized in that shower, and this will never be taken away from him. It is truly awesome how the Holy Spirit can be trusted to walk out the truth in our lives in full detail.

paradigm shift

My wife, Jenny, and I were invited to a feast. It was to be a tantalizing extravaganza of beef brisket slow-roasted over a mesquite grill. There would also be herb garlic chicken, garlic bread that had more butter and garlic than bread, and amazing fresh salad with feta cheese, sun dried tomatoes and croutons. The smells were intoxicating, the flavors were heavenly. We always enjoyed being at these kinds of festivals of food and family, whenever we were the privileged guest of any number of Italian families from within our church fellowship. You have to understand, these were real Italian families from the old country; second generation and absolutely looked the part.

A while back, one of these families started attending our church, first the wife, then the husband, who received Christ as his personal Lord and Savior. He was bought up in a strong loving Italian Catholic family. He had never had a real knowledge of a love relationship with God, through Christ, his Son. His complete life and heart had been changed. He found a new hope and joy in life, as his sins were forgiven, pure and simple, and his guilt was vanquished. The extended family experienced the difference. After this, his older brother began to investigate. Attending church a few times and checking things out, he asked me over to his house one time and ended up praying with me in his living room for him to follow Christ and know his love and grace. One family member after another came to see what was going on. Then other Italian friends started checking us out. *These guys were really connected.*

It was this group of family and friends who had come together for the feast to which we had been invited. These great loving people and fresh saints had gathered... and had included my wife and me, since I had the privilege of being their pastor and father in the faith. As in all Italian family gatherings (or

...that's
when I noticed
the
glasses...

at least the ones that I have been to) the respect and devotion to the "Father," or priest, is palpable. They loved and respected Jenny and me as they did the Pope.

As we sat down to this amazing meal, they asked if I would say a blessing over the meal. The banquet setting of fresh pasta, and platters of chicken, brisket, bread and salad were place on the grand old oak table, spread out before us in lavish abundance. The crowd gathered around with their olive-tan faces and full-hearted laughter. Each one was poised and hanging on my next words, heads bowed.

That's when I noticed... the glasses.

Each person had a glass of red wine at their place setting - including mine. This was a part of their whole meal. It was the Italian culture - food and wine. What was I to do as their pastor? I instantly had some serious internal conflicts arise in my heart and mind. I knew their heart was not wrong or rebellious; this was quite natural and the norm for them. Was this to be a teachable moment? Did these new believers need to hear the truth on the dangers of alcohol?

No, this was a teachable moment for me. I knew in my heart that if I, their pastor, their father in the faith, spoke to them at this time, they would, out of respect and honor, have obeyed my personal conviction about wine. They love me and would do what I ask of them without question. I was conflicted.

My mind was racing, for this new experience to me as a young pastor was but over time, something didn't add up

a personal challenge. This was not my background; this was completely foreign to me. The family I grew up in ate hamburgers, milk and casseroles. The family and church training I had received included the assumption that alcohol of any kind was not right in God's eyes. It was a sin. It always leads to drunkenness... and more sin. I was taught in my youth that Jesus did not turn the water into wine at the wedding, what he did was to turn the water into really excellent grape juice. The scriptures seemed perfectly clear that the use of any alcohol was forbidden.

"Don't be drunk with wine, because that will ruin your life. Instead, let the Holy Spirit fill and control you."
[Ephesians 5:18-19]

"Wine produces mockers; liquor leads to brawls. Whoever is led astray by drink cannot be wise."
[Proverbs 20:1]

But over time, something didn't add up. It became evident as I searched the scriptures in my late teen years, that the well-intentioned teaching I received was faulty. It was legalism and not based on solid application of the word of God.

I found out that Jesus did, in fact, turn that water into wine. Actually, it was wine of the highest quality. In addition, Jesus must have had wine himself, for he was accused of being part of that scene.

is there a shift anywhere in your thinking as you make your way through this book?

"And I, the Son of Man, feast and drink, and you say, 'He's a glutton and a drunkard, and a friend of the worst sort of sinners!' But wisdom is shown to be right by what results from it."
[Matthew 11:19]

The apostle Paul said to his student Timothy, a young pastor like me, that he should take some wine as a benefit to his health.

"Don't drink only water. You ought to drink a little wine for the sake of your stomach because you are sick so often."
[1 Timothy 5:23]

I was caught in a conflict. Wine is not sin, but the misuse of it is. How does this all work out? How can you know when it is a sin or it is not? How can we teach the truth in such a way as to give clear understanding which leads to life, and not a false understanding, as I had received, which brought to me, as well as others, both confusion and conflict of faith? So I took the time to wrestle out this process and the wisdom and insight from God came to the surface.

There is the Biblical core absolute that applies here and is found over and over in scripture, that wine, beer, alcohol or anything else should not have mastery over us. It is not the complete removal of alcohol from one's lifestyle, but the emphasis is that one should not get drunk or addicted to wine, beer or strong drink. For when this takes place, one's self control is lost and it gives place to the works of the flesh. We are to be filled with the Holy Spirit and submitted to God's leading, not being led by another "spirit."

we took the higher road
of love and respect, preferring
one another and applying
the BIBLICAL CORE
of truth.

Another important Biblical core truth is to be followed in this area as well. We are to honor and prefer one another, not causing a brother to stumble though the use of our choices. We are to be considerate of others and their possible areas of weakness, above our own freedoms, personal convictions, personal preferences or actions. We are to act in love so as to not bring an offense or stumbling block to another believer. Our actions and behavior should show the character of Christ and promote an authentic witness of Christ. We may personally have the freedom to partake or act at times, but it may be more prudent not to do so for the sake of another. A good guideline my mom taught me was that when in doubt, don't.

"You say,' I am allowed to do anything' - but not everything is good for you. and even though 'I am allowed to do anything,'- I must not become a slave to anything."
[1 Corinthians 6:12]

So the feast around the table that evening became a moment of personal maturity. Not only were the aromas, flavors and hospitality heavenly that evening, but so was its lesson. I didn't say anything to those precious people around the table that night about the wine, but we built a greater understanding by applying God's truth and heart with grace and confidence. We took the higher road of love and respect, preferring one another and applying the Biblical core of truth.

serious grace

Present day church leadership continues to bring about ugly confusion, toxic legalism and an unhealthy church culture when they choose to place personal convictions or traditions into the realm of the Biblical core. The issue of Christians attending these churches and losing passion and heart because of man-made religious weights is, of course, nothing new.

Amazingly, even in the early church, this was a major issue as well. Paul the Apostle was teaching and mentoring the people of Galatia, and he came upon this same problem, and it deeply affected the new believers and Christians of that local church. The Gentile believers of Galatia had come to faith through the life message and teaching of Paul. He related the Good News of the Gospel of Jesus, with insight and wisdom. He brought to them the foundation of understanding that these new Christ-followers were saved by faith, and by faith alone.

But Peter came along with other traditionally based Jewish teachers and told the church that the act of circumcision was a necessity. They proclaimed that this traditional act needed to be added to the experience of each follower in order to bring complete salvation to the believers found in Galatia.

These teachers of the Jewish law may have been coming with good intentions, as they proclaimed that to be fully accepted by Christ and a grafted part of God's people, one must be found in the same physical state as the Jewish believers. This was their tradition and personal conviction to be a true faithful follower of God. To them, circumcision was an outward sign of coming to faith, thus showing that the old skin of the flesh was cut away. But Paul made it very clear in his letter that the outward work of circumcision would not profit no human effort can bring about salvation

the Gentile believer. To the Gentile believer, this was just a man-made ritual without meaning or benefit to them. This tradition was only of value to those who lived with the understanding of the law, and Paul made a very strong case that since the law had been done away with by the covenant blood of Jesus, it was of no real "salvation" value to anyone.

The Gospel of Christ is this: Christ provides the change of heart needed in each one by personal repentance and placement of faith in Him. For God the Father is looking in each person for an authentic faith in Christ and the fruit of love following.

"For when we place our faith in Christ Jesus, it makes no difference to God whether we are circumcised or not circumcised. What is important is faith expressing itself in love."
[Galatians 5:6]

No outward action, such as circumcision, can change or make a heart right before God; only faith in the atoning work of Christ applied by His grace can accomplish that. No human effort can bring about salvation.

Circumcision did not bring the Jewish believers any closer to God, in reality. The obedience of Christ had served that purpose and fulfilled the entire requirement. Their act of conviction did not make a major pivotal difference in their overall relationship to God.   If it had, then Christ's work on the cross would only have been able to provide a partial salvation and cleansing.

what personal convictions must you keep outside the CORE and health for grace to flourish in your life?

"For if you are trying to make yourselves right with God by keeping the law, you have been cut off from Christ! You have fallen away from God's grace."
[Galatians 5:4]

The believers in Galatia were challenged by Paul to hold to the teaching and truth they had receive from him, to keep free in grace and relationship with Christ, by not taking on or making another's personal conviction or tradition their own Biblical core truth. They were to keep that on an outer circle. They were not to let it into the core, which would have brought about bondage and loss of grace and freedom.

"So Christ has really set us free. Now make sure that you stay free, and don't get tied up again in slavery to the law."
[Galatians 5:1]

For you and me today, the same is also true. Let us hold the Biblical core as our foundation and directive. By living from the core we can assure we will be fostering hope, health and wisdom within our lives. We will be experiencing grace and faith in our everyday love relationship with our Savior, and Lord, Jesus Christ. We will make sure that our convictions, which are well and good in their proper place, have no room in the core, but remain in the second circle, where they can be a support to the Biblical core.

When we can hold to this three circle categorization in the practice and actions of our personal life, good things will happen. We enjoy a genuine grace-based walk with Christ. We find a balance and security in knowing how and what it means to walk and live by the Spirit. Obeying and adhering laughter and joy exist because the people are not pinched by legalism or stifled by man-made rituals to the Biblical core truths releases us from condemnation and fear.

"For perfect love casts out fear."
[1 John 4:18]

When you add these well-balanced individuals into an active Christian community called a church, each one sharing the same core understanding and giving grace to each other's personal convictions, you release a community of believers with resilient health and power. An environment that heals and encourages will foster safety and promise. It is a soil where sustaining growth can flourish, with each new seed finding invigorating soft ground in which to grow, mercifully free of human rockiness. The very culture is sound. Laughter and joy exist because the people are not pinched by legalism or stifled by man-made rituals. The overall atmosphere is life-giving, loving, attractive and contagious.

Here are found real, authentic, genuine people who can be themselves...
enjoying a real God.

acknowledgements

I want to express my sincere thanks...

To the people of **Ross Valley Community Church** and **The Springs Church**, much of what is found in this book was because of the process and lessons we learned together. Thank you for allowing me proximity to your lives.

To **Joyce Erfert** and **Heather Gholson** for your great assistance in editing this text, boy did it need it.

To **the pastoral team** at The Springs Church. A big thanks goes to you for your prayers and encouragement. *"This is Church."*

To my **amazing and talented family** who challenged me to dream and put these ideas into print.

And to **Eric Huffman** who has taken the words on the page and crafted them into an expression of worship. For through your art, wordsmith and design you have truly brought this book to life.

Finally, and most importantly, my deepest thanks are to the grace and love of my **Savior, Jesus Christ**, you are **the core** of my existence.

the author

Mark Leuning has been a pastor for over 25 years.

He has planted two churches: one in Marin County, California; and his current church, The Springs Church, located in Chandler, Arizona.

As a gifted communicator with an ability to effectively reach and impact people of all ages, Mark has a passion to *love, mend, train and send* all people who find their way into the church, regardless of their starting condition, enabling them to go forth as leaders to live-out the message of hope.

Mark currently resides in the Phoenix Metro area with his beautiful wife Jennifer. Mark and Jenny have two adult married children: Janae and Tyler... and one amazing granddaughter, ZoëJane.

Some have found this material helpful in the formats of Pastor's Conferences and Retreats, Church Staff Workshops, One-Day Leadership Sessions and a Workshop for Creating a Vibrant Culture in the Church and Marketplace. Mark is willing to serve through these and other creative means of communication.

To get in touch with Mark for booking information or additional resources, and to order more books, go to:
www.3circlesbook.com

For more information about The Springs Church, check out:
www.thespringschurch.net